PROPAGANDA
OF THE DEED

Typesetting by Nathaniel Kennon Perkins

Published by Trident Press
940 Pearl St.
Boulder, CO 80302

tridentcafe.com

ISBN: 978-0-9992499-9-4

PROPAGANDA
OF THE DEED

———————

The Pocket Alexander Berkman

山

Trident Press
Boulder, CO

Contents

Editor's Introduction

It was July 23, 1892, and Alexander Berkman was planning to die. He just had some business to attend to first. Dressed in a new suit and a black derby hat, Berkman burst into the Pittsburg office of Henry Clay Frick, the notoriously anti-union manager of the Carnegie Steel Company. From his pocket, Berkman produced a pistol. He fired two shots before being tackled to the ground, at which point he managed to pull out a homemade dagger. He stabbed Frick three times. A carpenter who was working nearby heard the shots and the commotion, ran over, and smashed Berkman over the head with a hammer, stunning him. Berkman was arrested, and when police noticed that he was chewing on something, they retrieved a dynamite capsule from his mouth. He had planned to assassinate Frick and then kill himself.

During the two months that Berkman spent in jail awaiting his trial, Anarchists argued about the morality of his actions. Labor organizer Jo Labadie and individualist anarchist publisher Benjamin Tucker criticized the action, adamant that violence could only damage the anarchist cause. However, Emma Goldman and Lucy Parsons lauded him for this propaganda of the deed.

Propaganda of the deed is any specific political action meant to provide an example to others and thus serve as a catalyst for revolution. Such an act, if successful, is intended to demonstrate to the people that the state and ruling class are neither invincible nor omnipotent. Mikhail Bakunin wrote, "We must spread our principles, not with words but with deeds, for this is the most popular, the most potent, and the most irresistible of propaganda." There is an accelerationist motive here as well, encouraging reactive, repressive measures by the state and thereby expanding support for anarchist movements among the increasing number of oppressed and downtrodden.

Violence, in the form of assassination and terrorism, has been a common vehicle for this propaganda. Historian Beverly Gage discusses its justification by writing the following:

> Among anarchism's founding premises was the idea that capitalist society was a place of constant violence: every law, every church, every paycheck was based on force. In such a world, to do nothing, to stand idly by while millions suffered, was itself to commit an act of violence.

However, as Peter Kropotkin pointed out, "a structure based on centuries of history cannot be destroyed with a few kilos of dynamite." This is a lesson that we anarchists apparently have to learn over and over again. The very real brutality of state repression that followed any successful violent action in the late 19th and early 20th centuries has made the tactic increasingly unpopular. In 1911, Leon Trotsky noted, "The anarchist prophets of the 'propaganda by the deed' can argue all they want about the elevating and stimulating influence of terrorist acts on the masses; Theoretical considerations and political experience prove otherwise." Still, the philosophies behind such violence remain emotionally moving. This is why we keep throwing bricks through bank windows. We get to burn a cop car if we're lucky.

Of course, propaganda of the deed doesn't *require* violence. There are plenty of nonviolent applications, but I'm afraid they are as unlikely to spark revolution as violence is. Take for example, Daniel McGowan's extremely admirable Earth Liberation Front actions in 2001. Seven years in prison; no revolution yet.[1]

But that's more than enough cynicism. Back to how interesting Berkman is:

1. Watch the documentary *If a Tree Falls: A Story of the Earth Liberation Front* (Dir. Curry, 2011) for more on this.

At his trial, Berkman declined the services of a lawyer and represented himself against the advice of the warden.

He said, "I don't believe in your laws. I don't acknowledge the authority of your courts. I am innocent morally."

As an atheist, he refused to be sworn in.

The jury immediately found him guilty on all charges, and the judge handed down a sentence of 21 years in prison.

The years Berkman spent incarcerated involved extended periods in solitary confinement and the dungeon, homosexual affairs with fellow inmates, and multiple petitions denied by the board of pardons. He attempted escape in 1900. Comrades leased a house across the street from the prison with the intention of digging a tunnel from the basement and into the prison yard stable. They managed to do so in spite of the rocky soil and a leaking gas main that they disinterred. One comrade loudly sang and played piano to cover up the noise of the digging. However, on July 5 Berkman stole away to the stable only to find that heavy construction materials had been stacked there, blocking the entrance to the tunnel. A couple weeks later, a child playing in the yard of the then-abandoned house fell into the cellar and discovered the tunnel. Berkman tried to hang himself with his blanket in his cell.

Eventually, after serving 14 years of his sentence, Berkman was freed. He went on speaking tours, edited anarchist newspapers, organized, went back to prison, was deported, became disillusioned with the Russian Revolution, moved to Berlin, moved to Nice, became ill, and committed suicide by handgun on June 28, 1936.

Only a few weeks later, the Spanish Civil War started.

I think it's a person's right to die if they want to, but if Berkman's timing isn't an illustration of the best case against killing yourself, I don't know what is. Stick around. See what happens.

Berkman wrote some great books. These are *Prison Memoirs of an Anarchist*, *The Bolshevik Myth*, and *Now and After: The ABC of Communist Anarchism*. The book you hold in your hands contains a collection of his shorter works, mostly compiled from issues of *Mother Earth* and *The Blast*. Enjoy.

-Nathaniel Kennon Perkins
Boulder, CO, 2019

To the Youth of America

———

Tyranny must be opposed at the start.

Autocracy, once secured in the saddle, is difficult to dislodge.

If you believe that America is entering the war "to make democracy safe," then be a man and volunteer.

But if you know anything at all, then you should know that the cry of democracy is a lie and a snare for the unthinking. You should know that a republic is not synonymous with democracy, and that America has never been a real democracy, but that it is the vilest plutocracy on the face of the globe.

If you can see, hear, feel, and think, you should know that King Dollar rules the United States, and that the workers are robbed and exploited in this country to the heart's content of the masters.

If you are not deaf, dumb, and blind, then you know that the American bourgeois democracy and capitalistic civilization are the worst enemies of labor and progress, and that instead of protecting them, you should help to fight to destroy them.

If you know this, you must also know that the workers of America have no enemy in the toilers of other countries. Indeed, the workers of Germany suffer as much from their exploiters and rulers as do the masses of America.

You should know that the interests of Labor are identical in all countries. Their cause is international.

Then why should they slaughter each other?

The workers of Germany have been misled by their rulers into donning the uniform and turning murders.

So have the workers of France, of Italy, and England been misled.

But why should you, men of America,

allow yourselves to be misled into murder or into being murdered?

If your blood must be shed, let it be in defense of your own interests, in the war of the workers against their despoilers, in the cause of real liberty and independence.

Some Reminiscences
of Kropotkin

It was about 1890, when the anarchist movement was still in its infancy in America. We were just a handful then, young men and women fired by the enthusiams of a sublime ideal, and passionately spreading the new faith among the population of the New York Ghetto. We held our gatherings in an obscure hall in Orchard Street, but we regarded our efforts as highly successful. Every week greater numbers attended our meetings, much interest was manifested in the revolutionary teachings, and vital questions were discussed late into the night, with deep conviction and youthful vision. To most of us it seemed that capitalism had almost reached the limits of its fiendish possibilities, and that the Social Revolution was not far off. But there were many difficult questions and knotty problems involved in the growing movement, which we ourselves could not solve satisfactorily. We longed to have our great teacher Kropotkin among us, if only for a short visit, to have him clear up many complex points and to give us the benefit of his intellectual aid and inspiration. And then, what a stimulus his presence would be for the movement!

We decided to reduce our living expenses to the minimum and devote our earnings to defray the expense involved in our invitation to Kropotkin to visit America. Enthusiastically the matter was discussed in group meetings of our most active and devoted comrades; all were unanimous in the great plan. A long letter was sent to our teacher, asking him to come for a lecture tour to America and emphasizing our need of him.

His negative reply gave us a shock: we were so sure of his acceptance, so convinced of the necessity of his coming. But the admiration we felt for him was even increased when we learned the motives for his refusal. He would very much like to come — Kropotkin wrote — and he deeply appreciated the spirit of our invitation. He hoped to visit the United States sometime in the future, and it would give him great joy to be among such good comrades. But just now he could not afford to come at his own expense, and he would not use the money of the movement even for such a purpose.

I pondered over his words. His viewpoint was just, I thought, but it could apply only under ordinary circumstances. His case, however, I considered exceptional, and I deeply regretted his decision not to come. But his motives epitomized to me the man and the grandeur of his nature. I visioned him as my ideal of revolutionist and Anarchist.

Years later, while I was in the Western Penitentiary of Pensylvania, the hope of seeing our Grand Old man Kropotkin for a moment illumined the darkness of my cell. Friends had notified me that Peter had come to the States on his way to Canada, where he was to participate in some Congress of scientists. Peter intended to visit me, I was informed, and I counted the days and the hours waiting for the longed-for visit. Alas, the fates were against my meeting my teacher and comrade. Instead of being called to see my dear visitor, I was ordered into the Warden's office.* He held in his had a letter, and I recognised Peter's small and neat handwriting. On the envelope, after my name, Kropotkin had written, "Political Prisoner".

The Warden was in a rage. "We have no political prisoners in our free country!" he roared. And then he tore the envelope into pieces. I became enraged at such desecration. There followed a hot argument on American freedom in the course of which I called the Warden a liar. That was considered lese majesté and he demanded an apology. I refused. The result was that instead of meeting Peter I was sentenced to 7 days in the dungeon, which was a cell 2 feet by four, absolutely dark and 15 feet underground, one small slice of bread as my daily ration.

That was about the year 1895. In the years following Peter Kropotkin had repeatedly visited America, but I never got a chance to see him, because I was mostly in punishment in prison and for ten years I was deprived of visits and not allowed to see any one. A quarter of a century passed before I could at last take the hand of my old comrade in mine. It was in Russia, in March 1920, that I first met Peter. He lived in Dmitrov, a small town 60 verats from Moscow. I was in Petrograd (Leningrad) then, and the railroad conditions were such that traveling from the North to Dmitrov was out of the question. Later on I had a chance to go to Moscow and there I learned that the Government had made special arrangements to enable George Lansbury, the editor of the London Dail Herald, and one of his contributors, to visit Kropotkin in Dmitrov. I took advantage of the opportunity, together with our comrades Emma Goldman and A. Schapiro.

Meeting "celebrities" is generally disappointing: rarely does reality tally with the picture of our imagination. But it wasw not so in the case of Kropotkin; both physically and spiritually he corresponded almost exactly to the mental portrait I had made of him. He looked remarkably like his photographs, with his kindly eyes, sweet smile and generous beard. Every time Kropotkin entered the room it seemed to light up by his presence. The stamp of the idealist was so strikingly upon him, the spirirurality of his personality could almost be sensed. But I was schocked at the sight of his emaciation and feebleness.

Kropotkin received the academic pyock which was considerably better than the ration issued to the ordinary citizen. But it was far from sufficient to support life and it was a struggle to keep the wolf from the door. The question of fuel and lighting was also a matter of constant worry. The winters were severe and wood very scarce; kerosene difficult to procure, and it was considered a luxury to burn more than one lamp in the house. This lack was particularly felt by Kropotkin; it greatly handicapped his literary labors.

Several times the Kropotkin family had been dispossessed of their home in Moscow, their quarters being requisitioned for government purposes. They they decided to move to Dmitrov. It is only about half a hundred verats from the capital, but it might as well be a thousand miles away, so completely was Kropotkin isolated. His friends could rarely visit him; news from the Western world, scientific works, or foreign publications were unattainable. Naturally Kropotkin felt deeply the lack of intellectual companionship and mental relaxation.

I was eager to learn his views on the situation in Russia, but I soon realised that Peter did not feel free to express himself in the presence of the English visitors. The conversation was therefore of a general character. But one of his remarks was very significant and gave me the key to his attitude. "They have shown," he said, referring to the Bolsheviki, "how the Revolution is not to be made." I knew, of course, that as an Anarchist Kropotkin would not acept any Government position, but I wanted to learn why he was not participating in the economic up-building of Russia. Though old and physically weak, his advice and suggestions would be most valuable to the Revolution, and his influence of great advantage and encouragement to the Anarchist movement. Above all, I was interested to hear his positive ideas on the conduct of the Revolution. What I had heard so far from the revolutionary opposition was mostly critical, lacking helpful constructiveness.

The evening passed in desultory talk about the activities on the front, the crime of the Allied blokade in refusing even medicine to the sick, and the spread of disease resulting from lack of food and unhygenic conditions. Kropotkin looked tired, apparently exhausted by the mere presence of visitors. He was old and weak; and I feared he would not live much longer under those conditions. He was evidently undernourished, though he said that the Anarchists of the Ukraina had been trying to make his life easier by supplying him with flour and other products. Makhno, also, when still friendly with the Bolsheviki, had been able to send him provisions. Not to tire Peter too much, we left early.

Some months later I had another opportunity to visit our old comrade. It was summer-time and Peter seemed to have revived with the resurrection of Nature. He looked younger, in good health and full of youthful spirit. Without the presence of outsiders, like the former English visitors, he felt more at home with us and we talked freely about Russian conditions, his attitude and the outlook for the future. He was the genial Old Peter again, with a fine sense of humor, keen observation and most generous humanity. At first he chided me solemnly on my stand against the War, but he quickly changed the subject into less dangerous channels. Russia was our main point of discussion. The conditions were terrible, as everyone agreed, and the Dictatorship the greatest crime of the Bolsheviki. But there was no reason to lose faith, he assured me. The

Revolution and the masses were greater than any political Party and its machinations. The latter might triumph temporarily, but the heart of the Russian masses was uncorrupted and they would rally themselves to a clear understanding of the evil of the Dictatorship and of Bolshevik tyranny. Present Russian life, he said, was an artificial condition forced by the governing class. The rule of a small political Party was based on false theories, violent methods, fearful blunders and general inefficiency. They were suppressing the very expression of the people's will and initiative which alone could rebuild the ruined economic life of the country. The stupid attitude of the Allied Powers, the blockade and the attacks on the Revolution by the interventionists were helping to strengthen the power of the Communist regime. But things will change and the masses will awaken to the realisation that no one, no political Party or governmental clique must be permitted in the future to monopolise the Revolution, to control or direct it, for such attempts inevitably result in the death of the Revolution itself.

Various other phases of the Revolution we discussed on that occasion. Kropotkin particularly emphasised the constructive side of revolutions, and especially that the organisation of the economic life must be dealt with as the first and greatest necessity of a revolution, as the foundation of its existence and development. This thought he wanted to impress most forcibly upon our own comrades for our guidance in the coming great struggles of the international proletariat.

My visits to our dear Peter were a treat, intellectually and spiritually. I was leaving for the Ukraina for a long tour in behalf of the Petrograd Museum of the Revolution, but I hoped for many more visits to our old, brave teacher of the wonderful brain and heart. It was not to be. He died some months later, on February 8, 1921. I could reach his bedside in time only to say my last farewell to the dead. A great Man, a great Anarchist had departed.

The Need of Translating Ideals into Life

One year has passed since the death of Francisco Ferrer. His martyrdom has called forth almost universal indignation against the cabal of priest and ruler that doomed a noble man to death. The thinking, progressive elements throughout the world have voiced their protest in no ambiguous manner. Everywhere sympathy has been manifested for Ferrer, the modern victim of the Spanish Inquisition, and deep appreciation expressed for his work and aims. In short, the death of Ferrer has succeeded — as probably no other martyrdom of recent history — in rousing the social conscience of man. It has clarified the eternally unchanging attitude of the church as the enemy of progress; it has convincingly exposed the State as the crafty foe of popular advancement; it has, finally, roused deep interest in the destiny of the child and the necessity of rational education.

It would indeed be a pity if the intellectual and emotional energies thus wakened should exhaust themselves in mere indignation and unprofitable speculation concerning the unimportant details of Ferrer's personality and life. Protest meetings and anniversary commemorations are quite necessary and useful, in proper time and place. They have already accomplished, so far as the world at large is concerned, a great educational work. By means of these the social consciousness has been led to realize the enormity of the crime committed by the Church and State of Spain. But "the world at large" is not easily moved to action; it requires many terrible martyrdoms to disturb its equilibrium of dullness; and even when disturbed, it tends quickly to resume its wonted immobility. It is the thinking, radical elements which are, literally, the movers of the world, the intellectual and emotional disturbers of its stupid equanimity. They must never be suffered to become dormant, for they, too, are in danger of growing absorbed in mere adulation of the martyr and rhetorical admiration of his great work. As Ferrer himself has wisely cautioned us; "Idols are created when men are praised, and this is very bad for the future of the human race. The time devoted to the dead would be better employed in improving the condition of the living, most of whom stand in great need of this."

These words of Francisco Ferrer should be italicized in our minds. The radicals, especially, — of whatever creed — have much to atone for in this respect. We have given too much time to the dead, and not enough to the living. We have idealized our martyrs to the extent of neglecting the practical needs of the cause they died for. We have idealized our ideals to the exclusion of their application in actual life. The cause of it was an immature appreciation of our ideals. They were too sacred for everyday use. The result is evident, and rather discouraging. After a quarter of a century — and more — of radical propaganda, we can point to no very particular achievement. Some progress, no doubt, has been made; but by no means commensurate with the really tremendous efforts exerted. This comparative failure, in its turn, produces a further disillusioning effect: old-time radicals drop from the ranks, disheartened; the most active workers become indifferent, discouraged with lack of results.

It is this the history of every world-revolutionizing idea of our times. But especially is it true of the Anarchist movement. Necessarily so, since by its very nature it is not a movement that can conquer immediate tangible results, such as a political movement, for instance, can accomplish. It may be said that the difference between even the most advanced political movement, such as Socialism, and Anarchism is this: the one seeks the transformation of political and economic conditions, while the goal of the other includes a complete transvaluation of individual and social conceptions. Such a gigantic task is necessarily of slow progress; nor can its advancement be counted by noses or ballots. It is the failure to realize fully the enormity of the task that is partly responsible for the pessimism that so often overtakes the active spirits of the movement. To that is added the lack of clarity regarding the manner of social accoutrements.

The Old is to give birth to the New. How do such things happen? as little Wendla asks her mother in Wedekind's Frühlings Erwachen. We have outgrown the stork of Social Revolution that will deliver us the newborn child of ready-made equality, fraternity, and liberty. We now conceive of the coming social life as a condition rather than a system. A condition of mind, primarily; one based on solidarity of interests arising from social understanding and enlightened self-interest. A system can be organized, made. A condition must be developed. This development is determined by existing environment and the intellectual tendencies of the times. The causation of both is no doubt mutual and interdependent, but the factor of individual and propagandistic effort is not to be under-estimated.

The social life of man is a centre, as it were, whence radiate numerous intellectual tendencies, crossing and zigzagging, receding and approaching each other in interminable succession. The points of convergence create new centres, exerting varying influences upon the larger centre, the general life of humanity. Thus new intellectual and ethical atmospheres are established, the degree of their influence depending, primarily, on the active enthusiasm of the adherents; ultimately, on the kinship between the new ideal and the requirements of human nature. Striking this true chord, the new ideal will affect ever more intellectual centres which gradually begin interpreting themselves into life and transvaluing the values of the great general centre, the social life of man.

Anarchism is such an intellectual and ethical atmosphere. With sure hand it has touched the heart of humanity, influencing the world's foremost minds in literature, art, and philosophy. It has resurrected the individual from the ruins of the social debacle. In the forefront of human advance, its progress is necessarily painfully slow: the leaden weight of ages of ignorance and superstition hangs heavily at its heels. But its slow progress should by no means prove discouraging. On the contrary: it evidences the necessity of greater effort, of solidifying existing libertarian centres, and of ceaseless activity to create new ones.

The immaturity of the past had blinded our vision to the true requirements of the situation. Anarchism was regarded, even by its adherents, as an ideal for the future. Its practical application to current life was entirely ignored. The propaganda was circumscribed by the hope of ushering in the Social Revolution. Preparation for the new social life was not considered necessary. The gradual development and growth of the coming day did not enter into revolutionary concepts. The dawn had been overlooked. A fatal error, for there is no day without dawn.

The martyrdom of Francisco Ferrer will not have been in vain if, through it, the Anarchists — as well as other radical elements — will realize that, in social as well as in individual life, conception precedes birth. The social conception which we need, and must have, is the creation of libertarian centres which shall radiate the atmosphere of the dawn into the life of humanity.

Many such centres are possible. But the most important of all is the young life, the growing generation. After all, it is they upon whom will devolve the task of carrying the work forward. Just in the proportion that the young generation grows more enlightened and libertarian, will we approach a freer society. Yet in this regard we have been, and still are, unpardonably negligent; we Anarchists, Socialists, and other radicals. Protesting against the superstition-breeding educational system, we nevertheless continue to subject our children to its baneful influence. We condemn the madness of war, yet we permit our offspring to be inculcated with the poison of patriotism. Ourselves more or less emancipated from false bourgeois standards, we still suffer our children to be corrupted by the hypocrisy of the established. Every such parent directly aids in the perpetuation of dominant ignorance and slavery. Can we indeed expect a generation reared in the atmosphere of the suppressive, authoritarian educational régime, to form the cornerstone of a free, self-reliant humanity? Such parents are criminally guilty toward themselves and their children: they rear the ghost that will divide their house against itself, and strengthen the bulwarks of darkness.

No intelligent radical can fail to realize the need of the rational education of the young. The rearing of the child must become a process of liberation by methods which shall not impose ready-made ideas, but which should aid the child's natural self-unfoldment. The purpose of such an education is not to force the child's adaptation to accepted concepts. but to give free play to his [and her] originality, initiative, and individuality. Only by freeing education from compulsion and restraint can we create the environment for the manifestation of the spontaneous interest and inner incentives on the part of the child. Only thus can we supply rational conditions favorable to the development of the child's natural tendencies and his latent emotional and mental faculties. Such methods of education, essentially aiding the child's imitative quality and ardor for knowledge, will develop a generation of healthy intellectual independence. It will produce men and women capable, in the words of Francisco Ferrer, "of evolving without stopping, of destroying and renewing their environment without cessation; of renewing themselves also; always ready to accept what is best, happy in the triumph of new ideas, aspiring to live multiple lives in one life."

Upon such men and women rests the hope of human progress. To them belongs the future. And it is, to a very considerable extent, in our own power to pave the way. The death of Francisco Ferrer were in vain, our indignation, sympathy, and admiration worthless, unless we translate the ideals of the martyred educator into practice and life, and thus advance the human struggle for enlightenment and liberty.

A beginning has already been made. Several schools, along Ferrer lines, are being conducted in New York and Brooklyn; Philadelphia and Chicago are also about to open classes. At present the efforts are limited, for lack of aid and teachers, to Sunday schools. But they are the nucleus of grand, far-reaching potentiality. The radical elements of America, and chiefly the Francisco Ferrer Association, could rear no worthier nor more lasting monument to the memory of the martyred educator, Francisco Ferrer, than by a generous response to this appeal for the establishment of the first Francisco Ferrer Day School in America.

Prisons and Crime

Modern philanthropy has added a new role to the repertoire of penal institutions. While, formerly, the alleged necessity of prisons rested, solely, upon their penal and protective character, to-day a new function, claiming primary importance, has become embodied in these institutions — that of reformation.

Hence, three objects — reformative, penal, and protective — are now sought to be accomplished by means of enforced physical restraint, by incarceration of a more or less solitary character, for a specific, or more or less indefinite period.

Seeking to promote its own safety, society debars certain elements, called criminals, from participation in social life, by means of imprisonment. This temporary isolation of the offender exhausts the protective role of prisons. Entirely negative in character, does this protection benefit society? Does it protect?

Let us study some of its results.

First, let us investigate the penal and reformative phases of the prison question.

Punishment, as a social institution, has its origin in two sources; first, in the assumption that man is a free moral agent and, consequently, responsible for his demeanor, so far as he is supposed to be compos mentis; and, second, in the spirit of revenge, the retaliation of injury. Waiving, for the present, the debatable question as to man's free agency, let us analyze the second source.

The spirit of revenge is a purely animal proclivity, primarily manifesting itself where comparative physical development is combined with a certain degree of intelligence. Primitive man is compelled, by the conditions of his environment, to take the law into his own hands, so to speak, in furtherance of his instinctive desire of self-assertion, or protection, in coping with the animal or human aggressor, who is wont to injure or jeopardize his person or his interests. This proclivity, born of the instinct of self-preservation and developed in the battle for existence and supremacy, has become, with uncivilized man, a second instinct, almost as potent in its vitality as the source it primarily developed from, and occasionally even transcending the same in its ferocity and conquering, for the moment, the dictates of self-preservation.

Even animals possess the spirit of revenge. The ingenious methods frequently adopted by elephants in captivity, in avenging themselves upon some particularly hectoring spectator, are well known. Dogs and various other animals also often manifest the spirit of revenge. But it is with man, at certain stages of his intellectual development, that the spirit of revenge reaches its most pronounced character. Among barbaric and semi-civilized races the practice of personally avenging one's wrongs — actual or imaginary — plays an all-important role in the life of the individual. With them, revenge is a most vital matter, often attaining the character of religious fanaticism, the holy duty of avenging a particularly flagrant injury descending from father to son, from generation to generation, until the insult is extirpated with the blood of the offender or of his progeny. Whole tribes have often combined in assisting one of their members to avenge the death of a relative upon a hostile neighbor, and it is always the special privilege of the wronged to give the death-blow to the offender.

Even in certain European countries the old spirit of blood-revenge is still very strong. The semi-barbarians of the Caucasus, the ignorant peasants of Southern Italy, of Corsica and Sicily, still practice this form of personal vengeance; some of them, as the Tsherkessy, for instance, quite openly; others, as the Corsicans, seeking safety in secrecy. Even in our so-called enlightened countries the spirit of personal revenge, of sworn, eternal enmity, still exists. What are the secret organizations of the Mafia type, so common in all South European lands, but the manifestations of this spirit?! And what is the underlying principle of duelling in its various forms — from the armed combat to the fistic encounter — but this spirit of direct vengeance, the desire to personally avenge an insult or an injury, fancied or real; to wipe out the same, even with the blood of the antagonist. It is this spirit that actuates the enraged husband in attempting the life of the "robber of his honor and happiness." It is this spirit that is at the bottom of all lynch-law atrocities, the frenzied mob seeking to avenge the bereaved parent, the young widow or the outraged child.

Social progress, however, tends to check and eliminate the practice of direct, personal revenge. In so-called civilized communities the individual does not, as a rule, personally avenge his wrongs. He has delegated his "rights" in that direction to the State, the government; and it is one of the "duties" of the latter to avenge the wrongs of its citizens by punishing the guilty parties. Thus we see that punishment, as a social institution, is but another form of revenge, with the State in the role of the sole legal avenger of the collective citizen — the same well-defined spirit of barbarism in disguise. The penal powers of the State rest, theoretically, on the principle that, in organized society, "an injury to one is the concern of all"; in the wronged citizen society as a whole is attacked. The culprit must be punished in order to avenge outraged society, that "the majesty of the Law be vindicated." The principle that the punishment must be adequate to the crime still further proves the real character of the institution of punishment: it reveals the Old-Testamental spirit of "an eye for an eye, a tooth for a tooth," — a spirit still alive in almost all so-called civilized countries, as witness capital punishment: a life for a life. The "criminal" is not punished for his offence, as such, but rather according to the nature, circumstances and character of the same, as viewed by society; in other words, the penalty is of a nature calculated to balance the intensity of the local spirit of revenge, aroused by the particular offence.

This, then, is the nature of punishment. Yet, strange to say — or naturally, perhaps — the results attained by penal institutions are the very opposite of the ends sought. The modern form of "civilized" revenge kills, figuratively speaking, the enemy of the individual citizen, but breeds in his place the enemy of society. The prisoner of the State no longer regards the person he injured as his particular enemy, as the barbarian does, fearing the wrath and revenge of the wronged one. Instead, he looks upon the State as his direct punisher; in the representatives of the law he sees his personal enemies. He nurtures his wrath, and wild thoughts of revenge fill his mind. His hate toward the persons, directly responsible, in his estimation, for his misfortune — the arresting officer, the jailer, the prosecuting attorney, judge and jury — gradually widens in scope, and the poor unfortunate becomes an enemy of society as a whole. Thus, while the penal institutions on the one hand protect society from the prisoner so long as he remains one, they cultivate, on the other hand, the germs of social hatred and enmity.

Deprived of his liberty, his rights, and the enjoyment of life; all his natural impulses, good and bad alike, suppressed; subjected to indignities and disciplined by harsh and often inhumanely severe methods, and generally maltreated and abused by official brutes whom he despises and hates, the young prisoner, utterly miserable, comes to curse the fact of his birth, the woman that bore him, and all those responsible, in his eyes, for his misery. He is brutalized by the treatment he receives and by the revolting sights he is forced to witness in prison. What manhood he may have possessed is soon eradicated by the "discipline." His impotent rage and bitterness are turned into hatred toward everything and everybody, growing in intensity as the years of misery come and go. He broods over his troubles and the desire to revenge himself grows in intensity, his until then perhaps undefined inclinations are turned into strong anti-social desires, which gradually become a fixed determination. Society had made him an outcast; it is his natural enemy. Nobody had shown him either kindness or mercy; he will be merciless to the world.

Then he is released. His former friends spurn him; he is no more recognized by his acquaintances; society points its finger at the ex-convict; he is looked upon with scorn, derision, and disgust; he is distrusted and abused. He has no money, and there is no charity for the "moral leper." He finds himself a social Ishmael, with everybody's hand turned against him — and he turns his hand against everybody else.

The penal and protective functions of prisons thus defeat their own ends. Their work is not merely unprofitable, it is worse than useless; it is positively and absolutely detrimental to the best interests of society.

It is no better with the reformative phase of penal institutions. The penal character of all prisons — workhouses, penitentiaries, state prisons — excludes all possibility of a reformative nature. The promiscuous mingling of prisoners in the same institution, without regard to the relative criminality of the inmates, converts prisons into veritable schools of crime and immorality.

The same is true of reformatories. These institutions, specifically designed to reform, do as a rule produce the vilest degeneration. The reason is obvious. Reformatories, the same as ordinary prisons, use physical restraint and are purely penal institutions — the very idea of punishment precludes true reformation. Reformation that does not emanate from the voluntary impulse of the inmate, one which is the result of fear — the fear of consequences and of probable punishment — is no real reformation; it lacks the very essentials of the latter, and so soon as the fear has been conquered, or temporarily emancipated from, the influence of the pseudo-reformation will vanish like smoke. Kindness alone is truly reformative, but this quality is an unknown quantity in the treatment of prisoners, both young and old.

Some time ago I read the account of a boy, thirteen years old, who had been confined in chains, night and day for three consecutive weeks, his particular offence being the terrible crime of an attempted escape from the Westchester, N. Y., Home for Indigent Children (Weeks case, Superintendent Pierce, Christmas, 1895). That was by no means an exceptional instance in that institution. Nor is the penal character of the latter exceptional. There is not a single prison or reformatory in the United States where either flogging and clubbing, or the straight-jacket, solitary confinement, and "reduced" diet (semi-starvation) are not practiced upon the unfortunate inmates. And though reformatories do not, as a rule, use the "means of persuasion" of the notorious Brockway, of Elmira, N. Y., yet flogging is practiced in some, and starvation and the dungeon are a permanent institution in all of them.

Aside from the penal character of reformatories and the derogatory influence the deprivation of liberty and enjoyment exercise on the youthful mind, the associations in those institutions preclude, in the majority of cases, all reformation. Even in the reformatories no attempt is made to classify the inmates according to the comparative gravity of their offenses, necessitating different modes of treatment and suitable companionship. In the so-called reform schools and reformatories children of all ages — from 5 to 25 — are kept in the same institution, congregated for the several purposes of labor, learning and religious service, and allowed to mingle on the playing grounds and associate in the dormitories. The inmates are often classified according to age or stature, but no attention is paid to their relative depravity. The absurdity of such methods is simply astounding. Pause and consider. The youthful culprit who is such probably chiefly in consequence of bad associations, is put among the choicest assortment of viciousness and is expected to reform! And the fathers and mothers of the nation calmly look on, and either directly further this species of insanity or by their silence approve and encourage the State's work of breeding criminals. But such is human nature — we swear it is day-time, though it be pitch-dark; the old spirit of *credo quia absurdum est*.

It is unnecessary, however, to enlarge further upon the debasing influence those steeped in crime exert over their more innocent companions. Nor is it necessary to discuss further the reformative claims of reformatories. The fact that fully 60 per cent of the male prison population of the United States are graduates of "Reformatories" conclusively proves the reformative pretentions of the latter absolutely groundless. The rare cases of youthful prisoners having really reformed are in no sense due to the "beneficial" influence of imprisonment and of penal restraint, but rather to the innate powers of the individual himself.

Doubtless there exists no other institution among the diversified "achievements" of modern society, which, while assuming a most important role in the destinies of mankind, has proven a more reprehensible failure in point of attainment than the penal institutions. Millions of dollars are annually expended throughout the "civilized" world for the maintenance of these institutions, and notwithstanding each successive year witnesses additional appropriations for their improvement, yet the results tend to retrogade rather than advance the purports of their founding.

The money annually expended for the maintenance of prisons could be invested, with as much profit and less injury, in government bonds of the planet Mars, or sunk in the Atlantic. No amount of punishment can obviate crime, so long as prevailing conditions, in and out of prison, drive men to it.

Sacco and Vanzetti
(Coauthored with Emma Goldman)

———

The names of the "good shoe-maker and poor fish-peddler" have ceased to represent merely two Italian workingmen. Throughout the civilised world Sacco and Vanzetti have become a symbol, the shibboleth of Justice crushed by Might. That is the great historic significance of this twentieth century crucifixion, and truly prophetic, were the words of Vanzetti when he declared, "The last moment belongs to us — that agony is our triumph."

We hear a great deal of progress and by that people usually mean improvements of various kinds, mostly life-saving discoveries and labor-saving inventions, or reforms in the social and political life. These may or may not represent a real advance because reform is not necessarily progress.

It is an entirely false and vicious conception that civilisation consists of mechanical or political changes. Even the greatest improvements do not, in themselves, indicate real progress: they merely symbolise its results. True civilization, real progress consists in *humanising* mankind, in making the world a decent place to live in. From this viewpoint we are very far from being civilised, in spite of all the reforms and improvements.

True progress is a struggle against the inhumanity of our social existence, against the barbarity of dominant conceptions. In other words, progress is a spiritual struggle, a struggle to free man from his brutish inheritance, from the fear and cruelty of his primitive condition. Breaking the shackles of ignorance and superstition; liberating man from the grip of enslaving ideas and practices; driving darkness out of his mind and terror out of his heart; raising him from his abject posture to man's full stature — that is the mission of progress. Only thus does man, individually and collectively, become truly civilised and our social life more human and worth while.

This struggle marks the real history of progress. Its heroes are not the Napoleons and the Bismarcks, not the generals and politicians. Its path is lined with the unmarked graves of the Saccos and Vanzettis of humanity, dotted with the auto-da-fé, the torture chambers, the gallows and the electric chair. To those martyrs of justice and liberty we owe what little of real progress and civilization we have today.

The anniversary of our comrades' death is therefore by no means an occasion for mourning. On the contrary, we should rejoice that in this time of debasement and degradation, in the hysteria of conquest and gain, there are still men that dare defy the dominant spirit and raise their voices against inhumanity and reaction: That there are still men who keep the spark of reason and liberty alive and have the courage to die, and die triumphantly, for their daring.

For Sacco and Vanzetti died, as the entire world knows today, because they were Anarchists. That is to say, because they believed and preached human brotherhood and freedom. As such, they could expect neither justice nor humanity. For the Masters of Life can forgive any offense or crime but never an attempt to undermine their security on the backs of the masses. Therefore Sacco and Vanzetti had to die, notwithstanding the protests of the entire world.

Yet Vanzetti was right when he declared that his execution was his greatest triumph, for all through history it has been the martyrs of progress that have ultimately triumphed. Where are the Caesars and Torquemadas of yesterday? Who remembers the names of the judges who condemned Giordano Bruno and John Brown? The Parsons and the Ferrers, the Saccos and Vanzettis live eternal and their spirits still march on.

Let no despair enter our hearts over the graves of Sacco and Vanzetti. The duty we owe them for the crime we have committed in permitting their death is to keep their memory green and the banner of their Anarchist ideal high. And let no near-sighted pessimist confuse and confound the true facts of man's history, of his rise to greater manhood and liberty. In the long struggle from darkness to light, in the age-old fight for greater freedom and welfare, it is the rebel, the martyr who has won. Slavery has given way, absolutism is crushed, feudalism and serfdom had to go, thrones have been broken and republics established in their stead. Inevitably, the martyrs and their ideas have triumphed, in spite of gallows and electric chairs. Inevitably, the people, the masses, have been gaining on their masters, till now the very citadels of Might, Capital and the State, are being endangered. Russia has shown the direction of the further progress by its attempt to eliminate both the economic and political master. That initial experiment has failed, as all first great social revaluations require repeated efforts for their realisation. But that magnificent historic failure is like unto the martyrdom of Sacco and Vanzetti — the symbol and guarantee of ultimate triumph.

Let it be clearly remembered, however, that the failure of first attempts at fundamental social change is always due to the false method of trying to establish the New by Old means and practices. The New can conquer only *by means of its own new spirit.* Tyranny lives by suppression; Liberty thrives on freedom. The fatal mistake of the great Russian Revolution was that it tried to establish *new* forms of social and economic life on the old foundation of coercion and force. The entire development of human society has been away from coercion and government, away from authority towards greater freedom and independence. In that struggle the spirit of liberty has ultimately won out. In the same direction lies further achievement. All history proves it and Russia is the most convincing recent demonstration of it. Let us then learn that lesson and be inspired to greater efforts in behalf of a new world of humanity and freedom, and may the triumphant martyrdom of Sacco

and Vanzetti give us greater strength and
endurance in this superb struggle.

France: July, 1929

The Russian Tragedy
(A Review & An Outlook)

Foreword

We live at a time when two civilisations are struggling for their existence. Present society is at death grips with the New Ideal. The Russian Revolution was but the first serious combat of the two forces, whose struggle must continue till the final triumph of the one or of the other.

The Russian Revolution has failed — failed of its ultimate purpose. But that failure is a temporary one. In the point of revolutionising the thought and feeling of the masses of Russia and of the world, in undermining the fundamental concepts of existing society, and lighting the torch of faith and hope for the Better Day, the

Russian Revolution has been of incalculable educational and inspirational value to mankind.

Though the Russian Revolution failed to achieve its true goal, it will forever remain a most magnificent historic event. And yet — tremendous as it is — it is but an incident in the gigantic war of the two worlds.

That war will go on, is going on. In that war capitalism is already facing its doom. Yet more: with capitalism, centralised political government, the State, is also doomed, — and that is the most significant lesson of the Russian Revolution as I see it.

This pamphlet was recently published in the Dutch language, whereupon a Holland critic wrote to me: "You have failed to give the full lesson of the Russian Revolution".

I agree with him. It will require a great many volumes to give "the full lesson" of so tremendous an event as the Russian Revolution. My purpose is more modest. It will, require the effort of many minds to clarify to the world the full significance of the Russian Revolution, the potentiality ties of the ideals and ideas involved in it. I merely want to contribute my little share.

I have decided to incorporate the result of my two years' study and observation in Russia in a series of pamphlets under the general caption of the Russian Revolution Series.

The Series will comprise a critical review of the most important phases of the Revolution, together with a. constructive analysis of some of the vital lessons to be drawn.

If the present Series will help to make things a little clearer in regard to Russia, if it will aid the workers to see the path of liberation a little straighter, then I shall consider my effort fully repaid.

May, 1922

Alexander Berkman

I

It is most surprising how little is known, outside of Russia, about the actual situation and the conditions prevailing in that country. Even intelligent persons, especially among the workers, have the most confused ideas about the character of the Russian Revolution, its development, and its present political, economic and social status. Understanding of Russia and of what has been happening there since 1917 is most inadequate, to say the least. Though the great majority of people side either with or against the Revolution, speak for or against the Bolsheviki, yet almost nowhere is there concrete knowledge and clarity in regard to the vital subjects involved. Generally speaking, the views expressed — friendly or otherwise — are based on very incomplete and unreliable, frequently entirely false, information about the Russian Revolution, its history and the present phase of the Bolshevik regime But not only are the opinions entertained founded, as a rule, on insufficient or wrong data; too often they are deeply colored — properly speaking, distorted — by partisan feeling, personal prejudice, and class interests. On the whole, it is sheer ignorance, in one form or another, which characterises the attitude of the great majority of people toward Russia and Russian events.

And yet, understanding of the Russian situation is most vital to the future progress and wellbeing of the world. On the correct estimation of the Russian Revolution, the role played in it by the Bolsheviki and by other political parties and movements, and the causes that have brought about the present situation, — in short, on a thorough conception of the whole problem depends what lessons we shall draw from the great historic events of 1917. Those lessons will, for good or evil, affect the opinions and the activities of great masses of mankind. In other words, coming social changes — and the labor and revolutionary efforts preceding and accompanying them — will be profoundly, essentially influenced by the popular understanding of what has really happened in Russia.

It is generally admitted that the Russian Revolution is the most important historic event since the Great French Revolution. I am even inclined to think that, in point of its potential consequences, the Revolution of 1917 is the most significant fact in the whole known history of mankind. It is the only Revolution which aimed, de facto, at social world revolution; it is the only one which actually abolished the capitalist system on a country-wide scale, and fundamentally altered all social relationships existing till then. An event of such human and historic magnitude must not be judged from the narrow viewpoint of partisanship. No subjective feeling or preconception should be consciously permitted to color one's attitude. Above all, every phase of the Revolution must be carefully studied, without bias or prejudice, and all the facts dispassionately considered, to enable us to form a just and adequate opinion. I believe — I am firmly convinced — that only the whole truth about Russia, irrespective of any considerations whatever, can be of ultimate benefit.

Unfortunately, such has not been the case so far, as a general rule. It was natural, of course, for the Russian Revolution to arouse bitterest antagonism, on the one hand, and most passionate defense, on the other. But partisanship, of whatever camp is not an objective judge. To speak plainly, the most atrocious lies, as well as ridiculous fairy tales, have been spread about Russia, and are continuing to be spread, even at this late day. Naturally, it is not to be wondered at that the enemies of the Russian Revolution, the enemies of revolution, as such, the reactionaries and their tools, should have flooded the world with most venomous misrepresentation of events transpiring in Russia. About them and their "information" I need not waste any further words: in the eyes of honest, intelligent people they are discredited long ago.

But, sad to state, it is the would be friends of Russia and of the Russian Revolution who have done the greatest harm to the Revolution, to the Russian people, and to the best interests of the working masses of the world, by their exercise of zeal untempered by truth. Some unconsciously, out of ignorance, but most of them consciously and intentionally have been lying, persistently and cheerfully, in defiance of all facts, in the mistaken notion that they are "helping the Revolution". Reasons of "political expediency", of "Bolshevik diplomacy", of the alleged "necessity of the hour", and frequently motives of less unselfish considerations, have actuated them. The sole legitimate consideration of decent men, of real friends of the Russian Revolution and of man's emancipation, — As well as of reliable history — consideration for truth, they have entirely ignored.

There have been honorable exceptions, unfortunately too few: their voice has almost been lost in the wilderness of misrepresentation, falsehood, and overstatement. But most of those who visited Russia simply lied about the conditions in that country, — I repeat it deliberately. Some lied because they did not know any better: they had had neither the time nor the opportunity to study the situation, to learn the facts. They made "flying trips", spending ten days or a few weeks in Petrograd and Moscow, unfamiliar with the language, never for a moment coming in direct touch with the real life of the people, hearing and seeing only what was told or shown them by the interested officials accompanying them at every step. In many cases these "students of the Revolution" were veritable innocents abroad, naive to the point of the ludicrous. So unfamiliar were they with the environment that in most cases they had not even the faintest suspicion that their affable "interpreter", so eager to "show and explain everything", was in reality a member of the "trusted men", specially assigned to "guide" important visitors. Many such visitors have since spoken and written voluminously about the Russian Revolution, with little knowledge and less understanding.

Others there were who had the time and the opportunity, and some of them really tried to study the situation seriously, not merely for the purpose of journalistic "copy". During my two years' stay in Russia I had occasion to come in personal contact with almost every foreign visitor, with the Labor missions, and with practically every delegate from Europe, Asia, America and Australia, who gathered in Moscow to attend the, International Communist Congress and the Revolutionary Trade Union Congress held there last year. (1921.) Most of them could see and understand what was happening in the country. But it was a rare exception, indeed, that had vision and courage enough to realize that only the whole truth could serve the best interests of the situation.

As a general rule, however, the various visitors to Russia were extremely careless of the truth, systematically so, the moment they began "enlightening" the world. Their assertions frequently bordered on criminal idiocy. Think, for instance, of George Lansbury (publisher of the London "Daily Herald") stating that the ideas of brotherhood, equality, and love preached by Jesus the Nazarene were being realised in Russia — and that at the very time when Lenin was deploring the "necessity of military communism forced upon us by Allied intervention and blockade". Consider the "equality" that divided the population of Russia into 36 categories, according to the ration and wages received. Another Englishman, a noted writer, emphatically claimed that everything would be well in Russia, were it not for outside interference — while whole districts in the East, the South, and in Siberia, some of them larger in area than France, were in armed rebellion against the Bolsheviki and their agrarian policy. Other literati were extolling the "free Soviet system" of Russia, while 18,000 of her sons lay dead at Kronstadt in the struggle to achieve free Soviets.

But why enlarge upon this literary prostitution? The reader will easily recall to mind the legion of Ananiases who have been strenuously denying the very existence of the things that Lenin tried to explain as inevitable. I know that many delegates and others believed that the real Russian situation, if known abroad, might strengthen the hand of the reactionists and interventionists. Stith a belief, however, did not necessitate the painting of Russia as a veritable labor Eldorado. But the time when it might have been considered inadvisable to speak fully of the Russian situation is long past, That period has been terminated, relegated into the archives of history, by the introduction of the "new economic policy". Now the time has come when we must learn the full lesson of the Revolution and the causes of its debacle. That we may avoid the mistakes it made (Lenin frankly says they were many), that we be enabled to adopt its best features, we must know the whole truth about Russia.

It is therefore that I consider the present activities of certain labor men as positively criminal and a betrayal of the true interests of the workers of the world. I refer to the men and women, some of them delegates to the Congresses held in Moscow in 1921, that still continue to propagate the "friendly" lies about Russia, delude the masses with roseate pictures of labor conditions in that country, and even seek to induce workers of other lands to migrate in large numbers to Russia. They are strengthening the appalling confusion already existing in the popular mind, deceive the proletariat by false statements of the present and vain promises for the near future. They are perpetuating the dangerous delusion that the Revolution is alive and continuously active in Russia. It is most despicable tactics. Of course, it is easy for an American labor leader, playing to the radical element, to write glowing reports about the condition of the Russian workingmen, while he is being entertained at State expense at the Luxe, the most lucrative hotel in Russia. Indeed, he may insist that "no money is needed", for does he not receive everything his heart desires, free of charge? Or why should the President of an American needleworkers union not state that the Russian workers enjoy full liberty of speech? He is careful not to mention that only Communists and "trusties" were permitted within speaking distance while the distinguished visitor was "investigating" conditions in the factories.

May history be merciful to them.

II

That the reader may form a just estimate of what I shall say further, I think it necessary to sketch, briefly my mental attitude at the time of my arrival in Russia.

It was two years ago. A democratic government, "the freest on earth", had deported me — together with 248 other politicals — from the country I had lived in over thirty years. I had protested emphatically against the moral wrong perpetrated by an alleged democracy in resorting to methods it had so vehemently condemned on the part of the Tsarist autocracy. I branded deportation of politicals as an outrage on the most fundamental rights of man, and I fought it as a matter of principle.

But my heart was glad. Already at the outbreak of the February Revolution I had yearned to go to Russia. But the Mooney case had detained me: I was loath to desert the fight. Then I myself was taken prisoner by the United States, and penalised for my opposition to world slaughter. During two years the forced hospitality of the Federal penitentiary at Atlanta, Ga., prevented my departure. Deportation followed.

My heart was glad, did I say? Weak word to express the passion of joy that filled me at the certainty of visiting Russia. Russia! I was going to the country that had swept Tsardom off the map, I was to behold the land of the Social Revolution! Could there be greater joy to one who in his very childhood had been a rebel against tyranny, whose youth's unformed dreams had visioned human brotherhood and happiness, whose entire life was devoted to the Social Revolution?!

The journey was an inspiration. Though we Were prisoners, treated with military severity, and the "Buford" a leaky old tub repeatedly endangering our lives during the month's Odyssey, yet the thought that we were on the way to the land of revolutionary promise kept the whole company of deportees in high spirits, a tremble with expectation of the great Day soon to come. Long, long was the voyage, shameful the conditions we were forced to endure: crowded below deck, living in constant wetness and foul air, fed on the poorest rations. Our patience was nigh exhausted, yet our courage unflagging, and at last we reached our destination.

It was the 19th of January, 1920, when we touched the soil of Soviet Russia. A feeling of solemnity, of awe, almost overwhelmed me. Thus must have felt my pious old forefathers on first entering the Holy of Holies. A strong desire was upon me to kneel down and kiss the ground — the ground consecrated by the life-blood of generations of suffering and martyrdom, consecrated anew by the thriumphant [sic] revolutionists of my own day. Never before, not even when released from the horrible nightmare of 14 years' prison, had I been stirred so profoundly, — longing to embrace humanity, to lay my heart at its feet, to give my life a thousand times, were it but possible, to the service of the Social Revolution. It was the most sublime day of my life.

We were received with open arms. The revolutionary hymn, played by the military Red Band, greeted us enthusiastically as we crossed the Russian frontier. The hurrahs of the red-capped defenders of the Revolution echoed through the woods, rolling into the distance like threats of thunder. With bowed head I stood in the presence of the visible symbols of the Revolution Triumphant. With bowed head and bowed heart. My spirit was proud, yet meek with the consciousness of actual Social Revolution. What depths, what grandeur lay therein, what incalculable possibilities stretched in its vistas!

I heard the still voice of my soul: "May your past life have contributed, if ever so little, to the realisation of the great human ideal, to this, its successful be-ginning". And I became conscious of the great happiness it offered me: to do, to work, to help with every fiber of my being the complete revolutionary expression of this wonderful people. They had fought and won. They proclaimed the Social Revolution. It meant that oppression has ceased, that submission and slavery, man's twin curses, were abolished. The hope of generations, of ages, has at last been real-ised justice has been established upon the earth — at least upon that part of it that was Soviet Russia, and nevermore shall the precious heritage be lost.

But years of war and revolution have exhausted the country. There is suffering and hunger, and much need of stout hearts and willing hands to do and help. My heart sang for joy. Aye, I will give myself fully, completely, to the service of the people; I shall be rejuvenated and grow young again in ever greater effort, in the hardest toil, for the furtherance of the common weal. My very life will I consecrate to the realisation of the world's great hope, the Social Revolution.

At the first Russian army outpost a massmeeting was held to welcome us. The large hall crowded with soldiers and sailors, the nun-dressed women on the speaker's platform, their speeches, the whole atmosphere palpitating with Revolution in action — all made a deep impression on me. Urged to say something, I thanked the Russian comrades for their warm welcome of the American deportees, congratulated them on their heroic struggle, and expressed my great joy at being in their midst. And then my whole thought and feeling fused in one sentence. "Dear Comrades", I said, "we came not to teach but to learn; to learn and to help".

Thus I entered Russia. Thus felt my fellow deportees

I remained two years. What I learned, I learned gradually, day by day, in various parts of the country. I had exceptional opportunities for observation and study. I stood close to the leaders of the Communist Party, associated much with the most active men and women, participated in their work, and travelled extensively through the country under conditions most favorable to personal contact with the life of the workers and peasants. At first I could not believe that what I saw was real. I would not believe my eyes, my ears, my judgment. As those trick mirrors that make you appear dreadfully monstrous, so Russia seemed to reflect the Revolution as a frightful perversion. It was an appalling caricature of the new life, the world's hope. I shall not now go into detailed description of my first impressions, my investigations, and the long process that resulted in my final conviction. I fought relentlessly, bitterly, against myself. For two years I fought. It is hardest to convince him who does not want to be convinced. And, I admit, I did not want to be convinced that the Revolution in Russia had become a mirage, a dangerous deception. Long and hard I struggled against this conviction. Yet proofs were accumulating, and each day brought more damning testimony. Against my will, against my hopes, against the holy fire of admiration and enthusiasm for Russia which burned within me, I was convinced — convinced that the Russian Revolution had been done to death.

How and by whom?

III

It has been asserted by some writers that Bolshevik accession to power in Russia was due to a coup de main, and doubt has been expressed regarding the social nature of the October change.

Nothing could be further from the truth. As a matter of historic fact, the great event known as the October Revolution was in the profoundest sense a social revolution. It was characterised by all the essentials of such a fundamental change. It was accomplished, not by any political party, but by the people themselves, in a manner that radically transformed all the heretofore existing economic, political and social relations. But it did not take place in October. That month witnessed only the formal "legal sanction" of the

revolutionary events that had preced-
ed it. For weeks and months prior to it,
the actual Revolution had been going on
all over Russia: the city proletariat was
taking possession of the shops and factories, while the peasants expropriated the
big estates and turned the land to their
own use. At the same time workers' com-
mitees, peasant committes and Soviets
sprang up all over the country, and there
began the gradual transfer of power from
the provisional government to the Soviets. That took place, first in Petrograd,
then in Moscow, and quickly spread to the
Volga region, the Ural district, and to Siberia. The popular will found expression
in the slogan, "All power to the Soviets",
and it went sweeping through the length
and breadth of the land. The people had
risen, the actual Revolution was on. The
keynote of the situation was struck by the
Congress of the Soviets of the North, pro-
claiming: "The provisional government of
Kerensky must go; the Soviets are the sole
power!"

That was on October 10th Practically all the real power was already with the Soviets. In July the Petrograd uprising against Kerensky was crushed, but in August the influence of the revolutionary workers and of the garrison was strong enough to enable them to prevent the attack planned by Korniloff. The Petrograd Soviet gained strength from day to day. On October 16th it organised its own Revolutionary Military Committee, an act of definance [sic] of and open challenge to the government. The Soviet, through its Revolutionary Military Committee, prepared to defend Petrograd against the coalition government of Kerensky and the possible attack of General Kaledin and his counter-revolutionary cossacks On October 22nd the whole proletarian population of Petrograd, solidarically supported by the garrison, demonstrated throughout the city against the government and in favor of "All power to the Soviets".

The All-Russian Congress of Soviets was to open on October 25th. The provisional government, knowing its very existence in imminent peril, resorted to drastic action. On October 23rd the Petrograd Soviet ordered the Kerensk Cabinet to withdraw within 48 hours. Driven to desperation, Kerensky undertook — on October 24th — to suppress the revolutionary press, arrest the most prominent revolutionists of Petrograd, and remove the active Commissars of the Soviet. The government relied on the "faithful" troops and on the young yunkers of the military student schools. But it was too late: the attempt to sustain the government failed. During the night of October 24–25 (November 6–7) the Kerensky government was dissolved — peacefully, without bloodshed — and the exclusive supremacy of the Soviets was established. The Communist Party stepped into power. It was the political culmination of the Russian Revolution.

IV

Various factors contributed to the success of the Revolution To begin with, it met with almost no active opposition:

the Russian bourgeoisie was unorganised weak, and not of a militant disposition. But the main reasons lay in the all-absorbing enthusiasm with which the revolutionary slogans had fired the whole people. "Down with the war!", "Immediate peace!", "The land to the peasant, the factory to the workers!", "All power to the Soviets!" — these were expressive of the passionate soul cry and deepest needs of the great masses. No power could withstand their miraculous effect.

Another very potent factor was the unity of the various revolutionary elements in their opposition to the Kerensky government. Bolsheviki Anarchists, the left faction of the Social:: Revolutionist party, the numerous politicals freed from prison and Siberian exile, and the hundreds of returned revolutionary emigrants, had all worked during the February-October months toward a common goal.

But if "it was easy to begin" the Revolution, as Lenin had said in one of his speeches, to develop it, to carry it to its logical conclusion was another and more difficult matter. Two conditions were essential to such a consummation: continued unity of all the revolutionary forces, and the application of the country's goodwill initiative and best energies to the important work of the new social construction. It must always be remembered — and remembered well — that revolution does not mean destruction only. It means destruction plus construction, with the greatest emphasis on the plus. Most unfortunately, Bolshevik principles and methods were soon fated to prove a handicap, a drawback upon the creative activities of the masses.

The Bolsheviki are Marxists. Though in the October days they had accepted and proclaimed anarchist watchwords (direct action by the people, expropriation, free Soviets, and so forth), it was not their social philosophy that dictated this attitude. They had felt the popular pulse — the rising waves of the Revolution had carried them far beyond their theories. But they remained Marxists. At heart they had no faith in the people and their creative initiative. As social-democrats they distrusted the peasantry, counting rather upon the support of the small revolutionary minority among the industrial element. They had advocated the Constituent Assembly, and only when they were convinced that they would not have a majority there, and therefore not be able to take State power into their own hands, they suddenly decided upon the dissolution of the Assembly, though the step was a refutation and a denial of fundamental Marxist principles. (Incidentally, it was an Anarchist, Anatoly Zheleznyakov in charge of the palace guard, who took the initiative in the matter). As Marxists, the Bolsheviki insisted on the nationalisation of the land: ownership, distribution and control to be in the hands of the State. They were in principle opposed to socialisation, and only the pressure of the Left faction of the Social-Revolutionists (the Spiridonova-Kamkov wing) whose influence among the peasantry was traditional, forced the Bolsheviki to "swallow the agrarian programme of the Socialist-Revolutionists whole", as Lenin afterwards put it.

From the first days of their accession to political power the Marxist tendencies of the Bolsheviki began to manifest themselves, to the detriment of the Revolution. Social-Democratic distrust of the peasantry influenced their methods and measures. At the All-Russian Conferences the peasants did not receive equal representation with the industrial workers. Not only the village speculator and exploiter, but the agrarian population, as a whole was branded by the Bolsheviki as "petty bosses" and "bourgeois", "unable to keep step with the proletariat on the road to socialism". The Bolshevik government discriminated against the peasant representatives in the Soviets and at the National Conferences, sought to handicap their independent efforts, and systematically narrowed the scope and activities of the Land Commissariat, then by far the most vital factor in the reconstruction of Russia. (The Commissariat was then presided over by a Left Social-Revolutionist).

Inevitably this attitude led to much dissatisfaction on the part of the great peasant masses. The Russian muzhik is simple and naive, but with the instinct of the primitive man he quickly senses a wrong: no fine dialectics can budge his once settled conviction. The very cornerstone of the marxian credo, the dictatorship of the proletariat, served as an affront and an injury to the peasantry. They demanded an equal share in the organisation and administration of the affairs of the country. Had they not been enslaved, oppressed and ignored long enough? The dictatorship of the proletariat the peasant resented as discrimination against himself. "If dictatorship must be", he argued, "why not of all who labor, of the town worker and of the peasant, together?"

Then came the Brest-Litovsk peace. In its far-reaching results it proved the death blow to the Revolution. Two months previously, in December, 1917, Trotzky had refused, with a fine gesture of noble indignation, the peace offered by Germany on conditions much more favorable to Russia. "We wage no war, we sign no peace!" he had said, and revolutionary Russia applauded him. "No compromise with German imperialism, no concessions", echoed through the length and breadth of the country, and the people stood ready to defend their Revolution to the very death, But now Lenin demanded the ratification of a peace that meant the most mean-spirited betrayal of the greater part of Russia, Finland, Latvia, Lithuania, Ukraina, White Russia, Bessarabia — all were to be turned over to the oppression and exploitation of the German invader and of their own bourgeoisie. It was a monstrous thing — the sacrifice at once of the principles of the Revolution and of its interests as well.

Lenin insisted on ratification, on the ground that the Revolution needed a "breathing spell", that Russia was exhausted, and that peace would enable the "revolutionary oasis" to gather strength for new effort. Radek denounced acceptance of Brest-Litvosk conditions as betrayal of the October Revolution. Trotzky disagreed with Lenin. The revolutionary forces split. The Left Social-Revolutionists, most of the Anarchists and many of the nonpartisan revolutionary elements were bitterly opposed to making peace with imperialism, especially on the terms dictated then by Germany. They declared that such a peace would be fatal to the Revolution; that the principle of "peace without annexations" must not be sacrificed; that the German conditions involved the basest treachery to the workers and peasants of the provinces demanded by the Prussians; that the peace would subject the whole of Russia to economic and political dependence upon German Imperialism, that the invaders would possess themselves of the Ukrainan bread and the Don coal, and drive Russia to industrial ruin.

But Lenin's influence was potent. He prevailed. The Brest-Litvosk treaty was ratified by the 4th Soviet Congress.

It was Trotzky who first asserted in refusing the German peace terms offered in December, 1917, that the workers and peasants, inspired and armed by the Revolution, could by guerilla warfare overcome any army of invasion. The Left Social-Revolutionists now called for peasant uprisings to oppose the Germans, confident that no army could conquer the revolutionary ardor of a people fighting for the fruits of their great Revolution. Workers and peasants, responding rushed to the aid of Ukraina and White Russia, then valiantly struggling against the German invaders. Trotzky ordered the Russian army to pursue and suppress these partisan units.

The killing of Mirbach followed. It was the protest of the Left Social-Revolutionists Party against, and the defiance of, Prussian imperialism within Russia. The Bolshevik government initiated repressive measures: it now felt itself, as it were, under obligations to Germany. Dzerzhinsky, head of the All-Russian Extraordinary Commission, demanded the delivery of the terrorist. It was a situation unique in revolutionary annals: a revolutionary party in power demanding of another revolutionary party, with which it had till then cooperated the arrest and punishment of a revolutionist for executing the representative of an imperialist government! The Brest-Litvosk peace had put the Bolsheviki in the anomalous position of a gendarme for the Kaiser. The Left Social-Revolutionists replied to Dzerzhinsky' demand by arresting the latter. This act, and the armed skirmishes which followed it (though insignificant in themselves) were thoroughly exploited by the Bolsheviki politically. They declared that it was an attempt of the Left Social-Revolutionist Party to seize the reins of government. They announced that party outlawed, and their extermination began.

These Bolshevik methods and tactics were not accident al. Soon it became evident that it is the settled policy of the Communist State to crush every form of expression not in accord with the government. After the ratification of the Brest-Litvosk peace the Left Social-Revolutionist Party withdrew its representative in the Soviet of People's Commissars

The Bolsheviki thus remained in exclusive control of the government. Under one pretext and another there followed most arbitrary and cruel suppression of all the other political parties and movements. The Mensheviki and the Right Social-Revolutionists had been "liquidated" long before, together with the Russian bourgeoisie. Now was the turn of the revolutionary elements — the Left Social-Revolutionists the Anarchists, the non-partisan revolutionists.

But the "liquidation" of these involved much more than the suppression of small political groups. These revolutionary elements had strong followings, the Left Social-Revolutionists among the peasantry, the Anarchists mainly among the city proletariat. The new Bolshevik tactics encompassed systematic eradication of every sign of dissatisfaction, stifling all criticism and crushing independent opinion or effort. With this phase the Bolsheviki enter upon the dictatorship over the proletariat, as it is popularly characterised in Russia. The government's attitude to the peasantry is now that of open hostility. More increasingly is violence resorted to. Labor unions are dissolved, frequently by force, when their loyalty to the Communist Party is suspected. The cooperatives are attacked. This great organisation, the fraternal bond between city and country, whose economic functions were so vital to the interests of Russia and of the Revolution, is hindered in its important work of production, exchange and distribution of the necessaries of life, is disorganised, and finally completely abolished.

Arrests, night searches, zassada (house blockade), executions, are the order of the day. The Extraordinary Commissions (Tcheka), originally organised to fight counter-revolution and speculation, is becoming the terror of every worker and peasant. Its secret agents are everywhere, always unearthing "plots", signifying the razstrel (shooting) of hundreds without hearing, trial or appeal. From the intended defense of the Revolution the Tcheka becomes the most dreaded organisation, whose injustice and cruelty spread terror over the whole country. All-powerful, owing no one responsibility, the Tchecka is a law unto itself, possesses its own army, assumes police, judicial, administrative and executive powers, and makes its own laws that supersede those of the official State. The prisons and concentration camps are filled with alleged counter-revolutionists and speculators, 95 per cent of whom are starved workers, simple peasants, and even children of 10 to 14 years of age. (See reports of prison investigations, Petrograd "Krasnaya Gazetta" and "Pravda"; Moscow "Pravda", May, June, July, 1920). Communism becomes synonymous in the popular mind with Tchekism, the latter the epitome of all that is vile and brutal. The seed of counter-revolutionary feeling is sown broadcast.

The other policies of the "revolutionary government" keep step with these developments. Mechanical centralisation, run mad, is paralising the industrial and economic activities of the country. Initiative is frowned upon, free effort systematically discouraged. The great masses are deprived of the opportunity to shape the policies of the Revolution, or take part in the administration of the affairs of the country. The government is monopolising every avenue of life: the Revolution is divorced from the people. A bureaucratic machine is created that is appalling in its parasitism, inefficiency and corruption. In Moscow alone this new class of sovburs (Soviet bureaucrats) exceeds, in 1920, the total of office holders throughout the whole of Russia under the Tsar in 1914. (See official report of investigation by Commitee of Moscow Soviet, 1921). The Bolshevik economic policies, effectively aided by this bureaucracy, completely disorganise the already crippled industrial life of the country. Lenin, Zinoviev, and other Communist leaders thunder philippics against the new Soviet bourgeoisie, — and issue ever new decrees that strengthen and augment its numbers and influence.

The system of yedinolitchiye is introduced: management by one person. Lenin himself is its originator and chief advocate. Henceforth the shop, and factory committees are to be abolished, stripped of all power. Every mill, mine, and factory, the railroads and all the other industries are to be managed by a single head, a "specialist", — and the old Tsarist bourgeoisie is invited to step in. The former bankers, bourse operators, mill owners and factory bosses become the managers, in full control of the industries, with absolute power over the workers. They are vested with authority to hire, employ and discharge the "hands", to give or deprive them of the payok (food ration), even to punish them and turn them over to the Tcheka. The workers, who had fought and bled for the Revolution and were willing to suffer, freeze and starve in its defense, resent this unheard of imposition. They regard it as the worst betrayal. They refuse to be dominated by the very owners and foremen whom they had driven, in the days of the Revolution, out of the factories and who had been so lordly and brutal to them. They have no interest in such a reconstruction. The "new system", heralded by

Lenin as the savior of the industries, results in the complete paralysis of the economic life of Russia, drives the workers en masse from the factories, and fills them with bitterness and hatred of everything "socialistic". The principles and tactics of Marxian mechanisation of the Revolution are sealing its doom.

The fanatical delusion that a little conspirative group, as it were, could achieve a fundamental social transformation proved the Frankenstein of the Bolsheviki. It led them to incredible depths of infamy and barbarism. The methods of such a theory, its inevitable means, are twofold: decrees and terror. Neither of these did the Bolsheviki spare. As Bukharin, the foremost ideologue of the militant Communists taught, terrorism is the method by which capitalistic human nature is to be transformed into fit Bolshevik citizenship. Freedom is "a bourgeois prejudice" (Lenin's favorite expression), liberty of speech and of the press unnecessary, harmful. The central government is the depository of all knowledge and wisdom.

It will do everything. The sole duty of the citizen is obedience. The will of the State is supreme.

Stripped of fine phrases, intended mostly for Western consumption, this was and is the practical attitude of the Bolshevik government. This government, the real and only actual government of Russia, consists of five persons, members of the inner circle of the Central Committee of the Communist Party of Russia. These "Big Five" are omnipotent. This group, in its true essence conspiratory, has been controlling the fortunes of Russia and of the Revolution since the Brest-Litvosk peace. What has happened in Russia since, has been in strict accord with the Bolshevik interpretation of Marxism. That Marxism, reflected through the Communist inner circle's megalomania of omniscience and omnipotence, has achieved the present debacle of Russia.

In consonance with their theory, the social fundamentals of the October Revolution have been deliberately destroyed. The ultimate object being a powerfully centralised State, with the Communist Party in absolute control, the popular initiative and the revolutionary creative forces of the masses had to be eliminated. The elective system was abolished, first in the army and navy, then in the industries. The Soviets of peasants and worker's were castrated and transformed into obedient Communist committees, with the dreaded sword of the Tcheka ever hanging over them. The labor unions government alised, their proper activities suppresed, they were turned into mere transmitters of the orders of the State. Universal military service, coupled with the death penalty for conscientious objectors; enforced labor, with a vast officialdom for the apprehension and punishment of, "deserters"; agrarian and industrial conscription of the peasantry; military Communism in the cities and the system of requisitioning in the country, characterised by Radek as simply grain plundering (International Press Correspondence, English edition, vol. 1, No. 17); the suppression of workers' protests by the use of the military;

the crushing of peasant dissatisfaction with an iron hand, even to the extent of whipping the peasants and razing their villages with artillery — (in the Ural, Volga and Kuban districts, in Siberia and the Ukraina) — this characterised the attitude of the Communist State toward the people, this comprised the "constructive social and economic policies" of the Bolsheviki.

Still the Russian peasants and workers, prizing the Revolution for which they had suffered so much, kept bravely fighting on numerous military fronts. They were defending the Revolution, as they thought. They starved, froze, and died by the thousands, in the fond hope that the terrible things the Communists did would soon cease. The Bolshevik horrors were, somehow — the simple Russian thought — the inevitable result of the powerful enemies "from abroad" attacking their beloved country. But when the wars will at last be over — the people naively echoed the official press — the Bolsheviki will surely return to the revolutionary path they entered in October, 1917, the path the wars had forced them temporarily to forsake.

The masses hoped and — endured. And then, at last, the wars were ended. Russia drew an almost audible sigh of relief, relief palpitating with deep hope. It was the crucial moment: the great test had come. The soul of a nation was a-quiver. To be or not to be? And then full realisation came. The people stood aghast. Repressions continued, even grew worse. The piratical razvyorstka, the punitive expeditions against the peasants, did not abate their murderous work. The Tcheka was unearthing more "conspiracies", executions were taking place as before. Terrorism was rampant. The new Bolshevik bourgeoisie lorded it over the workers and the peasants, official corruption was vast and open, huge food supplies were rotting through Bolshevik inefficiency and centralised State monopoly, — and the people were starving.

The Petrograd workers, always in the forefront of revolutionary effort, were the first to voice their dissatisfaction and protest. The Kronstadt sailors, upon investigation of the demands of the Petrograd proletariat, declared themselves solidaric with the workers. In their turn they announced their stand for free Soviets, Soviets free from Communist coercion, Soviets that should in reality represent the revolutionary masses and voice their needs. In the middle provinces of Russia, in the Ukraina, on the Caucasus, in Siberia, everywhere the people made known their wants, voiced their grievances, informed the government of their demands. The Bolshevik State replied with its usual argument : the Kronstadt sailors were decimated, the "bandits" of Ukraina massacred, the "rebels" of the East laid low with machine guns,

This done, Lenin announced at the X. Congress of the Communist Party of Russia (March, 1921) that his former policies were all wrong. The razvyorstka, the requisition of food, was pure robbery. Military violence against the peasantry a "serious mistake". The workers must receive some consideration. The Soviet bureaucracy is corrupt and criminal, a huge parasite. "The methods we have been using have failed." The people, especially the rural population, are not yet up to the level of Communist principles. Private ownership must be re-introduced free trade established. Henceforth the best Communist is he who can drive the best bargain. (Lenin's expression).

V

Back to Capitalism!

The present situation in Russia is most anomalous. Economically it is a combination of State and private capitalism. Politically it remains the "dictatorship of the proletariat" or, more correctly, the dictatorship of the inner circle of the Communist Party.

The peasantry has forced the Bolsheviki to make concessions to it. Forcible requisitioning is abolished. Its place has taken the tax in kind, a certain percentage of the peasant produce going to the government. Free trade has been legalised, and the farmer may now exchange or sell his surplus to the government, to the re-established co-operatives or on the open market. The new economic policy opens wide the door of exploitation. It sanctions the right of enrichment and of wealth accumulation. The farmer may now profit by his successful crops, rent more land, and exploit the labor of those peasants who have little land and no horses to work it with. The shortage of cattle and bad harvests in some parts of the country have created a new class of "farm hands" who hire themselves out to the well-to-do peasant. The poor people migrate from those regions which are suffering from famine and swell the ranks of this class. The village capitalist is in the making.

The city worker in Russia today, under the new economic policy, is in exactly the same position as in any other capitalistic country. Free food distribution is abolished except in a few industries operated by the government, The worker is paid wages, and must pay for his necessaries — as in any country. Most of the industries, in so far as they are active, have been let or leased to private persons. The small capitalist now has a free hand. He has a large field for his activities. The farmer's surplus, the product of the industries, of the peasant trades, and of all the enterprises of private ownership, are subject to the ordinary processes of business, can be bought and sold. Competition within the retail trade leads to incorporation and to the accumulation of fortunes in the hands of individuals.

Developing city capitalism and village capitalism can not long co-exist with "dictatorship of the proletariat". The unnatural alliance between the latter and foreign capitalism will in the near future prove another vital factor in the fate of Russia.

The Bolshevik government still strives to uphold the dangerous delusion that the "revolution is progressing", that Russia is "ruled by proletarian soviets", that the Communist Party and its State are identical with the people. It is still speaking in the name of the "proletariat". It is seeking to dupe the people with a new chimera. After awhile — the Bolsheviki now pretend — when Russia shall have become industrially resurrected, through the achievements of our fast growing capitalism, the "proletarian dictatorship" will also have grown strong, and we will return to nationalisation. The State will then systematically, curtail and supplant the private industries and thus break the power of the meanwhile developed bourgeoisie.

"After a period of partial denationalisation a stronger nationalisation begins", says Preobrazhensky, Finance Commissar, in his recent article, "The Perspectives of the New Economic Policy". Then will "Socialism be victorious on the entire front" (ibid). Radek is less diplomatic. "We certainly do not mean", he assures us in his political analysis of the Russian situation, entitled "Is the Russian Revolution a Bourgeois Revolution?" (I.P.C., Dec. 16, 1921) "that at the end of a year we shall again confiscate the newly accumulated goods. Our economic policy is based upon a longer period of time... We are consciously preparing ourselves for co-operating with the bourgeoisie; this is undoubtedly dangerous to the existence of the Soviet government, because the latter loses the monopoly on industrial production as against the peasantry. Does not this signify the decisive victory of capitalism? May we not then speak of our revolution as having lost its revolutionary character? ..."

To these very timely and significant questions Radek cheerfully replies with a categoric No! It is true, of course, as Marx taught, he admits, that economic relations determine the political ones, and that economic concessions to the bourgeoisie must lead also to political concessions. He remembers that when the powerful landowning class of Russia began making economic concessions to the bourgeoisie those concessions were soon followed by political ones and finally by the capitulation of the landowning class. But he insists that the Bolsheviki will retain their power even under the conditions of the restoration of capitalism. "The bourgeoisie is a historically deteriorating, dying class... That is why the working class (?)

of Russia can refuse to make political concessions to the bourgeoisie; since it is justified in hoping that its power will grow on a national and international scale more quickly than will the power of the Russian bourgeoisie".

Meanwhile, though authoritatively assured that his, "power is to grow on a national and international scale", the Russian worker is in a bad plight. The new economic policy has made the proletarian "dictator" a common, every-day wage slave, like his brother in countries unblessed with Socialist dictatorship. The curtailment of the government's national monopoly has resulted in the throwing of hundreds of thousands of men and women out of work. Many Soviet institutions have been closed; the remaining ones have discharged from 50 to 75 per cent of their employees. The large influx to the cities of peasants and villagers ruined by the razvyorstka, and those fleeing from the famine districts, has produced an unemployment problem of threatening scope. The revival of the industrial life through private capital is a very slow process, due to the general lack of confidence in the Bolshevik State and its promises.

But when the industries will again begin to function more or less systematically, Russia will face a very difficult and complex labor situation. Labor organisations, trade unions, do not exist in Russia, so far as the legitimate activities of such bodies are concerned. The Bolsheviki abolished them long ago. With developing production and capitalism, governmental as well as private, Russia will see the rise of a new proletariat whose interests must naturally come into conflict with those of the employing class. A bitter struggle is imminent. A struggle of a twofold nature: against the private capitalist, and against the State as an employer of labor. It is even probable that the situation may develop still another phase: antagonism of the workers employed in the State-owned industries toward the better-paid workers of private concerns. What will be the attitude of the Bolshevik government? The object of the new economic policy is to, encourage, in every way possible, the development of private enterprise and to accelerate the growth of industrialism. Shops, mines, factories and mills have already been leased to capitalists. Labor demands have a tendency to curtail profits; they interfere with the "orderly processes" of business. And as for strikes, they handicap production, paralise industry. Shall not the interests of Capital and Labor be declared solidaric in Bolshevik Russia?

The industrial and agrarian exploitation of Russia, under the new economic policy, must inevitably lead to the growth of a powerful labor movement. The workers' organisations will unite and solidify the city proletariat with the agrarian poor, in the common demand for better living conditions. From the present temper of the Russian worker, now enriched by his four years' experience of the Bolshevik regime, it may be assumed with considerable degree of probability that the coming labor movement of Russia will develop along syndicalist lines. The sentiment is strong among the Russian workers. The principles and methods of revolutionary syndicalism are not unfamiliar to them. The effective work of the factory and shop committees, the first to initiate the industrial expropriation of the bourgeoisie in 1917, is an inspiring memory still fresh in the minds of the proletariat. Even in the Communist Party itself, among its labor elements, the syndicalist idea is popular. The famous Labor Opposition, led by Shliapnikov and Mme. Kolontay within the Party, is essentially syndicalistic.

What attitude will the Bolshevik government take to the labor movement about to develop in Russia, be it wholly or even only partly syndicalistic? Till now the State has been the mortal enemy of labor syndicalism within Russia, though encouraging it in other countries. At the X. Congress of the Russian Communist Party (March, 1921) Lenin declared merciless warfare against the faintest symptom of syndicalist tendencies, and even the discussion of syndicalist theories was forbidden the Communists, on pain of exclusion from the Party. (See official Report,

X. Congress). A number of the Labor Opposition were arrested and imprisoned. It is not to be lightly assumed that the Communist dictatorship could satisfactorily solve the difficult problems arising out of a real labor movement under Bolshevik autocracy. They involve principles of Marxian centralisation, the functioning of trade or industrial unions independent of the omnipotent government, and active opposition to private capitalism. But not only the big and small capitalist will the workers of Russia soon have to fight. They will presently come to grips with State capitalism itself.

To correctly understand the spirit and character of the present Bolshevik phase, it is necessary to realise that the so-called "new economic policy" is neither new nor economic, properly considered. It is old political Marxism, the exclusive fountain-head of Bolshevik wisdom. As social-democrats they have remained faithful to their bible. Only a country where capitalism is most highly developed can have a social revolution — that is the acme of Marxian faith. The Bolsheviki, are about to apply it to Russia. True, in the October days of the Revolution they repeatedly deviated from the straight and narrow path of Marx. Not because they doubted the prophet. By no means. Rather that Lenin and his group, political opportunists, had been forced by irresistible popular aspiration to steer a truly revolutionary course. But all the time they hung on to the skirts of Marx, and sought every opportunity to direct the Revolution into Marxian channels. As Radek naively reminds us, "already in April, 1918, in a speech by comrade Lenin, the Soviet government attempted to define our next tasks and to point out the way which we now designate as the new economic policy". (I. P. C., Vol. 1,No. 17).

Significant admission! In truth, present Bolshevik policies are the continuation of the good orthodox Bolshevik Marxism of 1918. Bolshevik leaders now admit that the Revolution, in its post-October developments, was only political, not social. The mechanical centralisation of the Communist State — it must be emphasized — proved fatal to the economic and social life of the country. Violent party dictatorship destroyed the unity of the workers and the peasants, and created a perverted, bureaucratic attitude to revolutionary reconstruction. The complete denial of free speech and criticism, not only to the masses but even to the rank and file of the Communist Party itself, resulted in its undoing, through its own mistakes.

And now? Bolshevik Marxism is continuing in poor Russia But it is monstrously criminal to prolong this bloody Comedy of Errors. Communist construction is not possible alongside of a sickly capitalism, artificially developed. That capitalism can never be destroyed — as Lenin & Co. pretend to believe — by the regular processes of the Bolshevik State grown economically strong. The "new" policies are there fore a delusion and a snare, fundamentally reactionary. These policies themselves create the necessity for another revolution.

Must tortured humanity ever tread the same vicious circle?

Or will the workers at last learn the great lesson Of the Russian Revolution that every government, whatever its fine name and nice promises is by its inherent nature, as a government, destructive of the very purposes of the social revolution? it is the mission of government to govern, to subject, to strenghten and perpetuate itself. It is high time the workers learn that only their own organised, creative efforts, free from Political and State interference, can make their age-long struggle for emancipation a lasting success.

MORE VERY FINE TITLES FROM TRIDENT PRESS

Blood-Soaked Buddha/Hard Earth Pascal
by Noah Cicero

it gets cold by jasper avery

Major Diamonds Nights & Knives
by Katie Foster

Cactus by Nathaniel Kennon Perkins

Sixty Tattoos I Secretly Gave Myself at Work
by Tanner Ballengee

The Pocket Peter Kropotkin

The Pocket Emma Goldman

The Silence is the Noise by Bart Schaneman

The Pocket Aleister Crowley

Los Espiritus by Josh Hyde

The Soul of Man Under Socialism
by Oscar Wilde

www.ingramcontent.com/pod-product-compliance
Lightning Source LLC
Chambersburg PA
CBHW051026030426
42336CB00015B/2745